Emilie Griffin

Romantic Inspirations

PIANO SOLOS

by Robert D. Vandall

Contents

Production: Gary Muhlbach
Printing: Johnson Printing

mp1404

WALTZ IN A MINOR

ROBERT D. VANDALL

Allegro, molto rubato (♩ = ca. 138)

21
a tempo
f dim. e rit.
p
mp
simile
26
mf
31
f
mf
36
a tempo
mp molto rit.
p
41
rit.
L.H. over

CONSOLATION

Allegretto, con molto rubato (𝅗𝅥 = ca. 88)

ROBERT D. VANDALL

17
mf cresc.
21
f cresc.
25
ff
29
molto dim. e rit.
5

a tempo
p
mp
simile

49
dim. e rit.
53
meno mosso
L.H.
pp
una corda
a tempo
58
rit.

HUNGARIAN DANCE

ROBERT D. VANDALL

cresc.
f
p
cresc.
f
Vivace (𝅗𝅥 = ca. 144)
R.H. 8va on repeat
p - mf
legato

loco
49
53
57
mf
61

Tempo I
65
f
p
69
cresc.
f
73
p
cresc.
77
f
Vivace
81
ff

INTERMEZZO

Allegretto, molto rubato (♩ = ca. 96)

ROBERT D. VANDALL

a tempo
p
cresc.
f
poco rit.
a tempo
mp
mf
molto dim. e rit.
Tempo I
mp
simile
poco rit.
a tempo
L.H.
poco rit.

ETUDE IN C MINOR

ROBERT D. VANDALL

Allegro (𝅗𝅥 = ca. 100)

17
a tempo
p
cresc.
21
25
f
dim.
29
p

mf
p
mf
p
8va
15ma
Adagio (𝅗𝅥 = ca. 60)
loco
rit.
8va
f
dim.
rit.
p

SCHERZO IN A MINOR

Allegro Scherzando (𝅗𝅥 = ca. 112)

ROBERT D. VANDALL

17
p
21
p
25
mf
p
mf
p
29
33
p

37
mf
41
p
45
mf
49
dim.
8va
pp

NORWEGIAN DANCE

Allegretto grazioso (♩. = ca. 72)

ROBERT D. VANDALL

cresc.
mf
p
rit.
a tempo
f
mf
mp
8va
p
rit. e dim.
pp

MOMENT MUSICAL

Allegretto (♩ = ca. 96)

ROBERT D. VANDALL

mp1404

25
p
simile
31
cresc.
mf
p
37
cresc.
rit.
a tempo
43
f

49
mp
mf
55
f
61
p
67
rit.

EVENING HYMN

Inspired by Robert Schumann's ***Nordisches Lied***

Lento

ROBERT D. VANDALL

MAZURKA IN A MAJOR

Allegro Vivace (♩ = ca. 144)

ROBERT D. VANDALL

a tempo
17
f
21
poco rit.
Prestissimo (♩ = ca. 208)
R.H. 8va on repeat
25
p
mf - mp
30
(rit. 2nd time)
Tempo I
loco
35
f

poco rit.
a tempo
p
poco rit.
ten.
a tempo
f
rit.

BARCAROLLE

ROBERT D. VANDALL

Piu mosso
rit.
mp
mf
p subito
rit.

Tempo I
mp
mf
dim.
rit.
pp

Character Pieces in the Romantic Era - *Study Notes*

New, short musical forms emerged during the 19th century expressing single moods or scenes defined by their descriptive titles. Virtually every romantic composer from Beethoven to Richard Strauss composed character pieces.

Barcarolle
Songs (barcarolles) sung by gondoliers as they navigated their boats through the canals of Venice were imitated by European composers. Numerous songs and instrumental works were inspired by these barcarolles. Most barcarolles have a 6/8 time signature although Frederic Chopin's famous *Barcarolle in F#* is in 12/8. Their rhythm reflects the motion of a boat on water. Felix Mendelssohn included three "Gondellied Venezianisches" in his *Songs Without Words*. Gabriel Faure is well known for his thirteen barcarolles composed between 1885 and 1916.

Consolation
Franz Liszt composed several introspective piano works which he titled *Consolation*. The music is generally lyrical and soothing as would be the tone of voice of someone 'consoling' a friend or family member.

Hungarian Dance
Johannes Brahms, along with most composers of the Romantic era, used elements of traditional folk music in his music. Brahms composed twenty-one *Hungarian Dances* for piano duet between the years 1846-1885. Franz Liszt also used Hungarian and Gypsy folk music in his fifteen *Hungarian Rhapsodies*.

Etude
This French word can be translated as 'study'. Composers have used this title for works which isolate and exploit a particular aspect of performance technique. Some etudes excercise technical aspects of playing an instrument while others celebrate musical aspects of performance. Composers in the Romantic era elevated piano etudes to the concert stage. Frederic Chopin's *Etudes, Op. 25* are well-known among pianists.

Intermezzo
Various composers of the Romantic era of music wrote pieces they called *Intermezzo*. Sometimes they were composed as movements 'between' movements in large works like symphonies. More commonly they were composed as independent piano pieces. Most are brief and lyrical in nature. Johannes Brahms composed the most well-known of this type of intermezzi. Four in opus 76 (1878) and fourteen pieces late in his life opus 116-119 (1892).

Mazurka
This dance emerged from near Warsaw in Poland. While all mazurkas have triple meter, there are various types of mazurkas. Frederic Chopin, born in Poland, was very influenced by the dance and wrote at least fifty mazurkas for piano. He expressed a wide variety of emotion in these works. Szymanowski, also a Polish composer, and Russian composers Glinka and Tchaikovsky, were also inspired to write mazurkas.

Moment Musical (French: Moment Musicaux)
These terms were invented by Franz Schubert's publisher (in Vienna) in 1828 to describe each of six piano pieces by Schubert. Schubert's melodic genius is obvious in these pieces. Sergei Rachmaninov wrote a set of six pieces with this title in 1896.

Norwegian Dance
Nationalism was popular among artists of the Romantic period. Edvard Grieg and various other composers used traditional folk tunes and dance melodies as inspiration for original compositions.

Scherzo
A piece, commonly in quick triple time, which is light and playful in character. Translated from the Italian, scherzo means 'joke.' The scherzo was frequently used as a substitute for a minuet (also in triple time) as a movement in larger works like sonatas or symphonies. Chopin's four scherzos are well-known extended works. All four are in a presto tempo and in 3/4 meter.

Waltz
Though it can be traced to Austrio-German beginnings in 1750s, the waltz became one of the most popular dances ever during the 1800s. Most every composer of the mid 19th century expressed themselves in the triple time of a waltz. The closeness of the dancers (couples) and the whirling motions made the dance controversial in its time. The Strauss family of musicians brought the waltz to new heights in Vienna. Frederic Chopin composed numerous waltzes displaying a great variety of speed and mood.

Hymns and Chorales
The great composers of the Romantic era composed numerous hymn tunes and chorales. The use of rich harmonies and careful attention to voice leading make them favored hymns to this day.

These study notes were prepared by Gary Muhlbach.